1,000,000 Books

are available to read at

www.ForgottenBooks.com

Read online
Download PDF
Purchase in print

ISBN 978-0-267-38207-1
PIBN 11336042

This book is a reproduction of an important historical work. Forgotten Books uses state-of-the-art technology to digitally reconstruct the work, preserving the original format whilst repairing imperfections present in the aged copy. In rare cases, an imperfection in the original, such as a blemish or missing page, may be replicated in our edition. We do, however, repair the vast majority of imperfections successfully; any imperfections that remain are intentionally left to preserve the state of such historical works.

Forgotten Books is a registered trademark of FB &c Ltd.
Copyright © 2018 FB &c Ltd.
FB &c Ltd, Dalton House, 60 Windsor Avenue, London, SW19 2RR.
Company number 08720141. Registered in England and Wales.

For support please visit www.forgottenbooks.com

1 MONTH OF FREE READING

at

www.ForgottenBooks.com

By purchasing this book you are eligible for one month membership to ForgottenBooks.com, giving you unlimited access to our entire collection of over 1,000,000 titles via our web site and mobile apps.

To claim your free month visit:
www.forgottenbooks.com/free1336042

* Offer is valid for 45 days from date of purchase. Terms and conditions apply.

English
Français
Deutsche
Italiano
Español
Português

www.forgottenbooks.com

Mythology Photography **Fiction**
Fishing Christianity **Art** Cooking
Essays Buddhism Freemasonry
Medicine **Biology** Music **Ancient Egypt** Evolution Carpentry Physics
Dance Geology **Mathematics** Fitness
Shakespeare **Folklore** Yoga Marketing
Confidence Immortality Biographies
Poetry **Psychology** Witchcraft
Electronics Chemistry History **Law**
Accounting **Philosophy** Anthropology
Alchemy Drama Quantum Mechanics
Atheism Sexual Health **Ancient History**
Entrepreneurship Languages Sport
Paleontology Needlework Islam
Metaphysics Investment Archaeology
Parenting Statistics Criminology
Motivational

THE KOBZAR
OF THE UKRAINE

The Kobzar of the Ukraine

Being Select Poems of
TARAS SHEVCHENKO

Done into English Verse with Biographical Fragments by
ALEXANDER JARDINE HUNTER

ЗБІРКА
ІВАНА ЛУЧКОВА

Printed in Winnipeg.

Published by Dr. A. J. Hunter,
Teulon, Man.

Copyright, Canada, 1922
by Dr. A. J. Hunter,
Teulon, Man.

Contents

	Page
Introduction	9

POEMS.

BALLADS:
The Monk	13
Hamaleia	21
The Night of Taras	30

TALE:
Naimechka; or The Servant	39

SOCIAL AND POLITICAL POETRY:
Caucasus	68
To the Dead	81
A Dream	96
The Bondwoman's Dream	106
To the Makers of Sentimental Idyls	109

POEMS OF EXILE:
A Poem of Exile	114
Memories of Freedom	120
Memories of Exile	123
Death of the Soul	124
Hymn of Exile	126

RELIGIOUS POEMS:
On the 11th Psalm	130
Prayers	132

EARLY POEMS:
Mighty Wind	136
The Water Fairy	138

HUMOROUS AND SATIRICAL:
Hymn of the Nuns	140
To the Goddess of Fame	141

	Page
PREDICTION AND FAREWELL:	
Iconoclasm	143
My Testament	144
BIOGRAPHICAL FRAGMENTS.	
Who Was Taras Shevchenko	11
The Cossacks	19
Kobzars	29
The Forming of a Life	36
A Father's Legacy	67
The Meaning of Serfdom	79
Freedom and Friends	94
A Triumphal March	103
Autocrat Versus Poet	112
Siberian Exile	118
Returning Home	127

THE KOBZAR OF THE UKRAINE

Illustrations

The decorations and illustrations in this book are meant to show something of Ukrainian art.

The artistic instincts of the peasant women find satisfaction largely in the working of embroidery, each district having its own characteristic types of design.

One of Shevchenko's favorite fancies was to compare his versification to the work of the girls and women embroidering their designs on their garments. He frequently speaks of himself as "embroidering verses."

It is a favorite device of Ukrainian book-makers to decorate their pages with miniature landscapes and little figures.

The frontispiece of the present work is a picture of Shevchenko in youth from an original painted by himself. On page 129 we see him as he looked after his return from exile.

LIFE

Born 1814, February 25.

24 years a serf,
9 years a freeman,
10 years a prisoner in Siberia,
3 1-2 years under police supervision.

Died 1861, February 26.

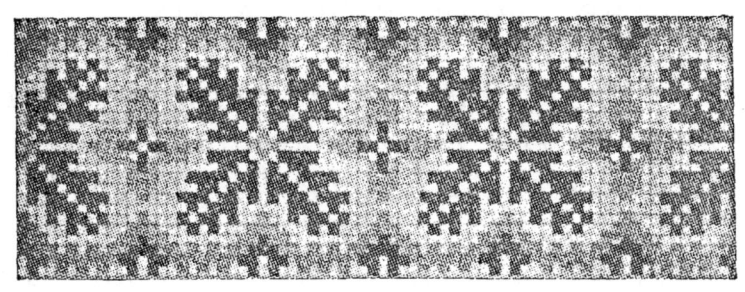

INTRODUCTION.

Nearly twenty years ago the translator of these poems was sent by the Presbyterian church as a medical missionary to a newly settled district in Manitoba. A very large proportion of the incoming settlers in this district were Ukrainians, indeed it was largely owing to the interest taken in these newcomers that the writer was sent there.

It was Mr. John Bodrug who first introduced him to the study of the poems of Shevchenko and with his help translations of three or four of the poems were made a dozen years ago. Press of other work prevented the following up of this study till last summer when with the help of Mr. Sigmund Bychinsky translations were made of the other poems here given, and considerable time spent in arriving at an understanding of the spirit of the poems and the nature of the situations described. Then the more formidable task was approached of trying to carry over not only the thought but some-

thing of the style, spirit and music of the original into the English tongue.

The spirit of Shevchenko was too independent to suffer him to be much bound by narrow rules of metre and rhyme. The translator has found the same attitude convenient, for when the versification may be varied as desired it is much easier to preserve the original thoughts intact.

The writer's thanks are due for help and advice to Messrs. Arsenych, Woicenko, Rudachek, Ferley, Sluzar and Stechyshyn and especially to Mrs. Bychinsky and for help with the manuscript to Miss Sara Livingstone.   A. J. H.

Who was Taras Shevchenko?

How many English-speaking people have heard of Taras Shevchenko?

What "Uncle Tom's Cabin" did for the negroes of the United States of America the poems of Shevchenko did for the serfs of Russia. They aroused the conscience of the Russian people, and the persecutions suffered by the poet at the hands of the autocracy awakened their sympathy.

It was two days after the death of Shevchenko that the czar's ukase appeared granting freedom to the serfs. Possibly the dying poet knew it was coming and died the happier on that account.

But in still another way does this man's figure stand out. In the country called the Ukraine is a nation of between thirty and forty millions of people, having a language of their own—the language in which these poems were composed.

This has been, as it were, a nation lost, buried alive one might say, beneath the power of surrounding empires.

They have a terrible history of oppression, alternating with desperate revolts against Polish and Muscovite tyranny.

In these poems speaks the struggling soul of a downtrodden people. To our western folk, reared in happier surroundings there is a bitter tang about some of them, somewhat like the taste of olives, to which one must grow accustomed. The Slavonic temperament, too, is given to melancholy and seems to dwell congenially in an atmosphere misty with tears. But he gravely misreads their literature who fails to perceive the grim resolve beneath the sorrow.

In the struggle of the Ukrainians for freedom the spirit of this poet, who was born a serf, remains ever their guiding star.

The Monk

It happened sometimes, when a cossack warrior found his energies failing and his joints growing stiff from much campaigning, he would bethink him of his sins and deeds of blood.

These things weighing on his mind, he would decide to spend the remainder of his life in a monastery, but before taking this irrevocable step, he would hold a time of high revel with his old comrades. This poem pictures such an event.

AT Kiev, in the low countrie,
Things happened once that you'll never
    see.
For evermore, 'twas done;
Nevermore, 'twill come.
Yet I, my brother,
Will with hope foregather,
That this again I'll see,
Though grief it brings to me.

To Kiev in the low countrie
Came our brotherhood so free.
Nor slave nor lord have they,
But all in noble garb so gay
Came splashing forth in mood full glad.
With velvet coats the streets are clad.
They swagger in silken garments pride
And they for no one turn aside.

In Kiev, in the low countrie,
All the cossacks dance in glee,
Just like water in pails and tubs
Wine pours out 'mid great hubbubs.
Wine cellars and bars
        with all the barmaids
The cossacks have bought
        with their wines and meads.
With their heels they stamp
    And dancing tramp,
While the music roars
    And joyously soars.

The people gaze
      with gladsome eyes,
While scholars of the cloister schools
All in silence bred by rules,
Look on with wondering surprise.
Unhappy scholars! Were they free,
They would cossacks dancing be.
Who is this by musicians surrounded
To whom the people give fame unbounded?
In trousers of velvet red,
With a coat that sweeps the road
A cossack comes. Let's weep o'er his years
For what they've done is cause for tears.
But there's life in the old man yet I trust,
For with dancing kicks
      he spurns the dust.
In his short time left with men to mingle
The cossack sings,
      this tipsy jingle.

"On the road is a crab, crab, crab.
Let us catch it grab, grab, grab.
Girls are sewing jab, jab, jab.
Let's dance on trouble,
Dance on it double
Then on we'll bubble.
Already this trouble
We-ve danced on double
So let's dance on trouble,
Dance on it double,
Then on we'll bubble."

To the Cloister of our Saviour
Old gray-hair dancing goes.
After him his joyous crowd
And all the folk of Kiev so proud.
Dances he up to the doors —
"Hoo-hoo! Hoo-hoo!" he roars.
Ye holy monks give greeting
A comrade from the prairie meeting.

    Opens the sacred door,
    The Cossack enters in.
    Again the portal closes
    To open no more for him.
    What a man was there
             this old gray-hair,
    Who said to the world farewell?
    'Twas Semon Palee,
             a cossack free
    Whom trouble could not quell.

Oh in the East the sun climbs high
And sets again in the western sky.
In narrow cell in monkish gown
Tramps an old man up and down,
Then climbs the highest turret there
To feast his eyes on Kiev so fair,
And sitting on the parapet
He yields a while to fond regret.
Anon he goes to the woodland spring,
The belfry near, where sweet bells ring.
The cooling draught to his mind recalls

How hard was life without the walls.
Again the monk his cell floor paces
'Mid the silent walls his life retraces.
The sacred book he holds in hand
And loudly reads,
The old man's mind to Cossack land
Swiftly speeds.
Now holy words do fade away,
The monkish cell turns Cossack den,
The glorious brotherhood lives again.
The gray old captain, like an owl
Peers beneath the monkish cowl.
Music, dances, the city's calls,
Rattling fetters, Moscow's walls,
O'er woods and snows
       his eyes can see
The banks of distant Yenisee.
Upon his soul deep gloom has crept
And thus the monk in sadness wept.

    Down, Down! Bow thy head;
    On thy fleshly cravings tread.
    In the sacred writings read.
    Read, read, to the ell give heed,
    Thy heart too long has ruled thee,
    All thy life it's fooled thee.
    Thy heart to exile led thee,
    Now let it silent be.
    As all things pass away,
    So thou shalt pass away.

Thus may'st thou know thy lot,
Mankind remembers not.

Though groans the old man's sadness tell,
Upon his book he quickly fell,
And tramped and tramped about his cell.
He sits again in mood forlorn
Wonders why he e'er was born.
One thing alone he fain would tell,
He loves his Ukraina well.
      For Matins now
          the great bell booms,
      The aged monk
          his cowl resumes.
      For Ukraina now to pray
      My good old Palee limps away.

The Cossacks

Back somewhere in the middle distance of European history—when the Ukraine was under Polish rule, though ever harrassed by the devastating raids of Turks and Tartars—there developed bands of guerilla fighters in the wild border-land beyond the rapids of the Dnieper.

Sometimes fighting against the Tartars, sometimes in alliance with them, they became known by the name 'Kazak,' a word of uncertain origin.

Fierce banditti they were, many of them serfs who had run away from their Polish masters. But they often developed great military power. At times the Poles succeeded in securing numbers of them as fighters in their army, but when the tyranny of the Polish landlords became intolerable the so-called "Registered Cossacks" would sometimes join with the "Free Cossacks" of the "border land"—which is the meaning of the word "Ukraine," and exact terrible vengeance on the Poles.

The story of these warlike deeds of the Cossacks has the same significance to the Ukrainian people that the tales of Wallace and Bruce have for Scotchmen.

THE KOBZAR OF THE UKRAINE

Cossacks Dictating a Saucy Letter to the Turkish Sultan.

Hamaleia

Hamaleia is an historical romance. The poet represents one of the excursions of the Zaporoggian Cossacks under the leadership of Hamaleia on Skutari, the Turkish city on the Bosphorus. The Cossacks saved western Europe from the Tartar and Turkish invasions, by fighting the invaders in the land of the barbarian. The poem describes one of these excursions where the Cossacks animated by the desire of revenging themselves on the Turks and freeing their brothers who were lying as captives in Turkish prisons, undertake a perilous trip in small wooden boats over the stormy Black Sea to Skutari, open the prisons, burn the city, and return home with rich spoils and their freed brethren.

OH breeze there is none,
  Nor do the waters run
From our Ukraina's land.
Perhaps, in council there they stand,
To march against the Turk demand.
We hear not in this foreign land.
Blow winds, blow across the sea,
Bring tidings of our land so free,
Come from Dnieper's Delta low,
Dry our tears and chase away our woe.

Roar in play thou sea so blue,
In yon boats are Cossacks true,
Their caps above are dimly seen.
Rescue for us this may mean.
Once more we'll hear Ukraina's story,
Once more the ancient Cossack glory
We'll hear before we die."

So in Skutari the Cossacks sang,
Their tears rolled down, their wailing rang.
Bosphorus groaned at the Cossack cry,
And then he raised his waves on high,
And shivering like a great grey bull,
His waters roaring far and full
Into the Black Sea's ribs were hurled.
The sea sent on great Bosphorus' cry,
To where the sands of the Delta lie,
And then the waters of Dnieper pale
In turn took up the mournful tale.

The father Dnieper rears his crest,
Shakes the foam from off his breast.
With laughter now aloud he calls
To spirits of the forest walls.
"Hortessa sister river, deep,
Time it is to wake from sleep.
Brother forest, sister river,
Come our children to deliver."
And now the Dnieper is clad with boats,
The Cossack song o'er the water floats.

    "In Turkey over there,
    Are wealth and riches rare.
    Hey, hey, blue sea play.
    Then roar upon the shore,
    Bringing with you guests so gay.

    "This Turkey has in her pockets
    Dollars and ducats.
    We don't come pockets to pick,
    Fire and sword will do the trick,
    We mean to free our brothers.

    "There the janissary crouches,
    There are pashas on soft couches.
    Hey-ho, foemen ware,
    For nothing do we care,
    Ours are liberty and glory."

    On they sail a-singing
    The sea to the wind gives heed.

In foremost boat the helm a-guiding,
Brave Hamaleia takes the lead.

"Oh, Hamaleia, our hearts are fainting,
Behold the sea in madness raving."
"Don't fear," he says, "these spurting
 fountains,
We'll hide behind the water mountains."

All slumber in the harem,
Byzantium's paradise.
Skutari sleeps, but Bosphorus
In madness shouts, "Arise!
Awake Byzantium!" it roars and groans.
"Awake them not, Oh Bosphorus."
Replies the sea in thunder tones.
"If thou dost I'll fill thy ribs with sand,
Bury thee in mud, change thee to solid land,
Perhaps thou knowest not the guest
I bring to break the sultan's rest."

So the sea insisted,
For he loved the brave Slavonic band;
And Bosphorus desisted,
While in slumber lay the Turkish land.
The lazy Sultan in his harem slept,
But only in Skutari the weary pris'ners wept.
For something are they waiting,
To God from dungeon praying,
While the waves go roaring by.

"Oh, loved God of Ukraine's land,
To us in prison stretch thy hand;

Slaves are we a Cossack band.
Shame it is now in truth to say,
Shame it will be at judgement day
For us from foreign tomb to rise,
And at thy court, to the world's surprise
Show Cossack hands in chains."
                      "Strike and kill,
Now the infidels will get their fill
Death to the unbelievers all."
How they scream beyond the wall!

They've heard of Hamaleia's fame.
Skutari maddens at his name.

"Strike on," he shouts, "kill and slay
To the castle break your way."
All the guns of Skutari roar
The foes in frenzy onward pour,
The cossacks rush with panting breath
The janissaries fall in death.

    Hamaleia in Skutari
    Dances through the flames in glee.
    To the jail his way he makes,
    Through the prison doors he breaks,
    Off the feet the fetters takes.

    "Fly away my birds so gray,
    In the town to share the prey."
    But the falcons trembled
    Nor their fears dissembled

So long they had not heard
A single christian word.

Night herself was frightened.
No flames her darkness lightened.
The old mother could not see
How the Cossacks pay their fee.

"Fear not! Look ahead,
To the Cossack banquet spread.
Dark over all, like a common day,
And this no little holiday."

"No sneak thieves with Hamaleia,
To eat their bacon silently
Without a frying pan."

"Let's have a light,"
Now burning bright
To heaven flames Skutari,
With all its ruined navy.

Byzantium awakes, its eyes it opens wide
With grinding teeth hastes to its
      comrade's side,
Byzantium roars and rages,
With hands to the shore it reaches,
From waters gasping strives to rise,
And then with sword in heart it dies.

With fires of hell Skutari's burning,
Bazaars with streams of blood are churning

Broad Bosphorus pours in its waves.
Like blackbirds in a bush
The Cossacks fiercely rush.
No living soul escapes.
Untouched by fire,
They the walls down tear,
Silver and gold in their caps they bear,
And load their boats with riches rare.

Burns Skutari, ends the fray,
The warriors gather and come away,
Their pipes with burning cinders light,
And row their boats through waves flame
      bright.

THE KOBZAR OF THE UKRAINE

Kobzars

These are the wandering minstrels of the Ukraine.

They play on an instrument called the Kobza which somewhat resembles a mandolin. Often in former days they were old prisoners of war—too old to work—so their Turkish captors first blinded them and then set them at liberty.

Wandering among the villages, guided by some little boy, they earned their bread by singing folk-songs and hero-tales to the accompaniment of the Kobza.

Shevchenko published his book of poems with the title "Kobzar."

The Night of Taras

BY the road the Kobzar sat
    And on his kobza played.
Around him youths and maidens
Like poppy flowers arrayed.

So the Kobzar played and sang
Of many an old old story;
Of wars with Russian, Pole and Tartar
And the ancient Cossack glory.

He sang of the wars of Taras brave,
Of battle fought in the morning early,
Of the fallen Cossack's grass-grown grave
Till smiles and tears did mingle fairly.

———

"Once on a time the Hetmans ruled,
    It comes not back again;
In olden days we masters were
    This never comes again.
These glories of old Cossack lore
Shall be forgotten nevermore.

    Ukraine, Ukraine!
    Mother mine, Mother mine!

When I remember thee
How mournful should I be.

What has come of our Cossacks bold
With coats of velvet red?
What of freedom by fate foretold,
And banners the Hetmans led?

Whither is it gone?
In flames it went:
O'er hills and tombs,
The floods were sent.
The hills are wrapt
in silence grim,
On boundless sea
waves ever play;
The tombs gleam forth
with sadness dim;
O'er all the land
the foe holds sway.

Play on, oh sea,
Hills silent be:
Dance, mighty wind,
O'er all the land.
Weep, Cossack youth,
Your fate withstand.

Now who shall our adviser be?
Then out spake Naleweiko,
A Cossack bold was he,
After him Paulioha
Like falcon swift did flee.

THE KOBZAR OF THE UKRAINE

Out spake Taras Traselo
With bitter words and true,
"That they trampled on Ukraina
For sure the Poles shall rue."
Out spake Taras Traselo,
Out spake the eagle grey.
Rescue for the faith he wrought,
Well indeed the Poles he taught.
"Let's make an end of our woe.
Arise, my gentle comrades, all
Upon the Poles with blows we'll fall."

Three days of war
    did the land deliver,
From the Delta's shore
    to Trubail's river.
The fields are covered
    with dead, in course,
But weary now
    is the Cossack force.

Now the dirty Polish ruler
Was feeling very jolly,
Gathered all his lords together,
For a time of feast and folly.
Taras did his Cossacks gather
To have a little talk together.

    "Captains and comrades,
My children and brothers,

What are we now to do?
Our hated foes are feasting,
I want advice from you."

"Let them feast away,
    It's fine for their health.

When the sun descends,
Old night her counsel lends;
The Cossacks'll catch them,
    and all of their wealth."

The sun reclined beyond the hill
The stars shone out in silence still,
Around the Poles the Cossack host
Was gathering like a cloud;
So soon the moon stood in the sky
When roared the cannon loud.

Woke up the Polish lordlings,
To run they found no place.
Woke up the Polish lordlings,
The foe they could not face.
The sun beheld the Polish lordlings,
In heaps all o'er the place.
With red serpent on the water,
River Alta brings the word —
That black vultures after slaughter
May feast on many a Polish lord.

And now the vultures hasten
The mighty dead to waken

Together the Cossacks gather
Praise to God to offer.

While black vultures scream,
O'er the corpses fight.
Then the Cossacks sing
A hymn to the night;
That night of famous story
Full of blood and glory.
That night that put the Poles to sleep
The while on them their foes did creep.

Beyond the stream
   in open field
A burial mound
   gleams darkly:
Where the Cossack blood was shed
There grows the grass full greenly.

On the tomb a raven sits:
With hunger sore he's screaming.
Waiting near a Cossack weeps:
Of days of old he's dreaming."

The Kobzar ceased in sadness
His hands would no longer play:
Around him youths and maidens
Were wiping the tears away.
By the path the Kobzar makes his way,
To get rid of his grief he starts to play.
And now the youngsters are dancing gay,
And then he opes his lips to say:

"Skip off, my children,
To some nice warm corner,
Of griefs enough;
I'll no longer be mourner.

To the bar I'll go
        and find my good wife
And there we'll have
        the time of our life.
For so we'll drink away our woes
And make no end of fun of our foes."

The Forming of a Life

The little Taras was born a serf. His first memories are of a mother's love, of the kindness of an elder sister, and like a musical undertone to all his life—the consciousness of the wonderful beauty of Nature.

But soon another power of hideous aspect laid its grasp on the childish soul. It was the knowledge of slavery, a grim and horrible thing that was slowly but surely grinding out the lives of his parents, and that would surely, later, reach out for his own.

Yet even the system of serfdom may allow a little happiness to a child, still too young to work.

The little boy had been told that beyond the distant hills were iron pillars holding up the sky. At five years of age he set out to find these pillars. Some teamsters found him wandering on the steppe and brought him back to his home. But this incident marked the character of the boy as an idealist and a dreamer.

Then there was Grandfather John, the brave old man who, half a century before, had fought in the ranks of the Haidemaki who so nearly broke the Polish power. On a Sunday the wondering family would listen to the mighty voice ringing out in the little home—telling of ancient battles for freedom.

When Taras was seven years of age he lost his mother. His father was left with six children, and thought to improve matters by marrying a widow with three. Thereafter the miseries increased for little Taras who was hated by his stepmother.

The father lived a few years longer, and to him Taras owed the knowledge of reading, for though they were serfs and lived in a wretched hovel, the Shevchenko's prided themselves on having retained some elements of culture.

Our little hero, however, had a strange passion for drawing and painting and also for singing, and found some employment among the drunken painters, and church-singers of the village.

Later his master tried to make him work, but found the lad hopeless for anything but his beloved painting. Finally, he reached Petrograd in the suite of his master's son, where he was apprenticed to a decorator.

A famous man came upon a ragged boy sitting on a pail, in the Royal Gardens, in the moonlight, drawing a picture of a statue there. This was the beginning of a period of good fortune. The lad was introduced to some of the great men of the capital. His genius was recognized. A famous painter painted a picture that was raffled off for sufficient money to purchase the boy's freedom, and he was entered as a student in the Academy.

Naimechka or The Servant

Prologue.

ON a Sunday, very early,
    When fields were clad with mist
A woman's form was bending
'Mid graves by cloud wreaths kissed.
Something to her heart she pressed,
In accents low the clouds addressed.

"Oh, you mist and raindrops fine,
Pity this ragged luck of mine.
Hide me here in grassy meadows,
Bury me beneath thy shadows.
Why must I 'mid sorrows stray?
Pray take them with my life away.
In gloomy death would be relief,
Where none might know or see my grief.
Yet not alone my life was spent,
A father and mother my sin lament.
Nor yet alone is my course to run
For in my arms is my little son.
Shall I, then, give to him christian name,
To poverty bind, with his mother's shame?

This, brother mist, I shall not do.
I alone my fault must rue.
Thee, sweet son, shall strangers christen,
Thy mother's eyes with teardrops glisten.
Thy very name I may not know
As on through life I lonely go.
I, by my sin, rich fortune lost,
With thee, my son, to ill fate, was tossed.
Yet curse me not,
        for evils past.
My prayers to heaven
        shall reach at last.
The skies above
        to my tears shall bend,
Another fortune to thee I'll send."
Through the fields she sobbing went.
The gentle mist
        its shelter lent.
Her tears were falling
        the path along,
As she softly sang
        the widows song:

"Oh, in the field there is a grave
Where the shining grasses wave;
There the widow walked apart,
Bitter sorrow in her heart.
Poison herbs in vain she sought,
Whereby evil spells are wrought.
Two little sons
        in arms she bore

Wrapped around in
        dress she wore;
Her children to the river carried,
In converse with the water tarried:
'Oh, river Dunai, gentle river,
I my sons to thee deliver,
Thou'lt swaddle them
        and wrap them,
Thy little waves
        will lap them,
Thy yellow sands
        will cherish them,
Thy flowing waters
        nourish them.'

I.

ALL by themselves lived
      an old couple fond
In a nice little grove
      just by a millpond.
Like birds of a feather
Just always together,
From childhood the two of them
      fed sheep together,
Got married, got wealthy,
      got houses and lands,
Got a beautiful garden
      just where the mill stands,
An apiary full
      of behives like boulders.
Yet no children were theirs,
      and death at their shoulders.
Who will cheer their passing years?
Who will soothe their mortal fears?
Who will guard their gathered treasure
In loyal service find his pleasure?
Who will be their faithful son
When low their sands of life do run?

Hard it is a child to rear,
In roofless house 'mid want and fear.
Yet just as hard 'mid gathered wealth,
When death creeps on with crafty stealth,
And one's treasures good
      At end of life's wandering,
Are for strangers rude
      For mocking and squandering.

II.

ONE fine, Sunday,
        in the bright sunlight,
All dressed up
        in blouses white,
The old folks sat
        on the bench by the door;
No cloud in sky,
        What could they ask more?
All peace and love
        it seemed like Eden.
Yet angels above
        their hearts might read in,
A hidden sorrow,
        a gloomy mood
Like lurking beast
        in darksome wood.
In such a heaven
        Oh, do you see
Whatever could
        the trouble be?
I wonder now
        what ancient sorrow
Suddenly sprang
        into their morrow.
Was it quarrel
        of yesterday
Choked off, then
        revived today,
Or yet some newly sprouted ire
Arisen to set their heaven on fire?

Perchance they're called to go to God,
Nor longer dwell on earth's green sod.
Then who for them on that far way
Horses and chariot shall array?

"Anastasia, wife of mine,
Soon will come our fatal day,
Who will lay our bones away?"

"God only knows.
With me always was that thought
Which gloom into my heart has brought.
Together in years and failing health,
For what have we gathered
        all this wealth?"

"Hold a minute,
Hearest thou? Something cries
Beyond the gate—'tis like a child.
Let's run! See'st ought?
I thought something was there."
Together they sprang
And to the gate running;
Then stopped in silence wondering.

Before the stile
        a swaddled child.
Not bound tightly,
        just wrapped lightly,
For it was
        in summer mild,

And the mother
>with fond caress
Had covered it
>with her own last dress.
In wondering prayer
>stood our fond old pair.
The little thing
>just seemed to plead.
In little arms
>stretched out you'ld read
Its prayer,—
>in silence all.
No crying—just a little breath its call.
"See, 'Stasia!
What did I tell thee?
Here is fortune and fate for us;
No longer dwell we in loneliness.
Take it
>and dress it.
Look at it!
>Bless it!
Quick, bear it inside,
To the village I'll ride.
Its ours to baptize,
God-parents we need for our prize."
>In this world
>>things strangely run.
>There's a fellow
>>that curses his son,
>Chases him away from home,
>Into lonely lands to roam.

While other poor creatures,
With sorrowful features,
With sweat of their toiling
Must much money earn;
The wage of their moiling
Candles to burn.
Prayers to repeat,
The saints to entreat;
For children are none.
This world is no fun
The way things run.

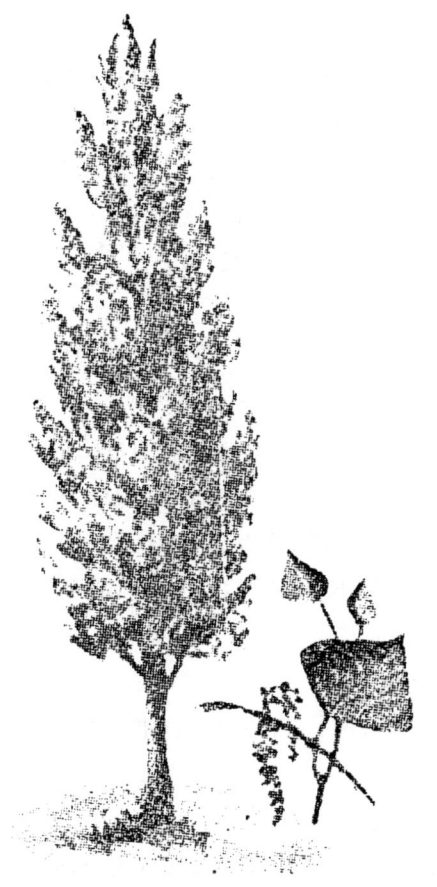

III.

THEIR joys do now such numbers reach
    God fathers and mothers
'Mid lots of others
Behold they have gathered
Three pairs of each.
At even they christen him,
And Mark is the name of him.

    So Mark grows,
    And so it goes.

For the dear old folk it is no joke,
For they don't know where to go,
Where to set him, when to pet him.
But the year goes and still Mark grows.
Yet they care for him, you'd scarce tell
    how,
Just as he were a good milk-cow.

And now a woman young and bright,
With eyebrows dark and skin so white,
Comes into this blessed place,
For servant's task she asks with grace.

"What, what—
    say we'll take her 'Stasia."

"We'll take her, Trophimus.
We are old and little wearies us;

He's almost grown within a year,
But yet he'll need more care, I fear."

"Truly he'll need care,
And now, praise God, I've done my share.
My knees are failing, so now
You poor thing, tell us your wage,
It is by the year or how?"

"What ever you like to give.'"

"No, no, it's needful to know,
It's needful, my daughter,
    to count one's wage.
This you must learn, count what you earn.
This is the proverb—
Who counts not his money
Hasn't got any.
But, child, how will this do?
You don't know us,
    We don't know you.
You'll stay with us a few days,
Get acquainted with our ways;
We'll see you day by day,
Bye and bye we'll talk of pay.
Is it so, daughter?"

"Very good, uncle."

"We invite you into the house."

And so they to agreement came.
The young woman seemed always the same,

Cheerful and happy as she'd married a lord
Who'd buy up villages just at her word.
She in the house and out doth work
From morning light to evening's mirk.

And yet the child is her special care;
Whatever befalls, she's the mother there.
Nor Monday nor Sunday this mother misses
To give its bath and its white dresses.
She plays and sings, makes waggons and things,
And on a holiday, plays with it all the day.

Wondering, the old folks gaze,
But to God they give the praise.

So the servant never rests,
But the night her spirit tests.
In her chamber then, I ween,
Many a tear she sheds unseen.
Yet none knows nor sees it all
But the little Mark so small.

Nor knows he why in hours of night
His tossings break her slumbers light.
So from her couch she quickly leaps,
The coverings o'er his limbs she keeps.
With sign of cross the child she blesses,
Her gentle care her love confesses.

Each morning Mark spreads out his hands
To the Servant as she stands;
Accepts, unknowing, a mother's care.
Only to grow is his affair.

IV.

MEANTIME many a year has rolled,
    Many waters to the sea have flowed,
Trouble to the home has come,
Many a tear down the cheek has run.
Poor old 'Stasia in earth they laid.
Hardly old Trophim' from death they saved.
The cursed trouble roared so loud,
And then it went to sleep, I trow.
From the dark woods where she frightened lay
Peace came back in the home to stay.

    The little Mark is farmer now.
    With ox-teams great in the fall must go
    To far Crimea to barter there
    Skins for salt and goods more rare.

    The Servant and Trophimus
        in counsel wise
    Plans for his marriage
        now devise.

    Dared she her thoughts utter
    For the Czar's daughter
    She'd send in a trice.
    But the most she could say
    While thinking this way
    Was, "Ask Mark's advice."

    "My daughter, we'll ask him,
    And then we'll affiance him."

So they gave' him sage advice,
And they made decision nice.

Soon his grave friends about him stand.
He sends them to woo, a stately band.
Back they come with towels on shoulder
Ere the day is many hours older.
The sacred bread they have exchanged,
The bargain now is all arranged.
They've found a maiden in noble dress.
A princess true, you well may guess.
Such a queen is in this affiance
As with a general might make alliance.
"Hail, and well done," the old man says,
And now let's have no more delays.
When the marriage, where the priest,
What about the wedding feast?
Who shall take the mother's place?
How we'll miss my 'Stasia's face."
The tears along his cheeks do fall,
Yet a word does the Servant's heart appall

Hastily rushing from the room,
In chamber near she falls in swoon.
The house is silent, the light is dim,
The sorrowing Servant thinks of him
And whispers: "Mother, mother, mother."

V.

ALL the week at the wedding cake
    Young women in crowds both mix and
        bake.
The old man is in wondrous glee,
With all the young women dances he.
At sweeping the yard
He labors hard.
All passers-by on foot and horseback
He hales to the court where is no lack
Of good home-brew.
All comers he asks to the marriage
And yet 'tis true
He runs around so
You'd not guess from his carriage
Though his joy is such a wonderful gift,
His old legs are 'most too heavy to lift.

Everywhere is disorder and laughter
Within the house and in the yard.
From store-room keg upon keg follows after,
Workers' voices everywhere heard.
They bake, they boil,
At sweeping toil,
Tables and floors they wash them all.

And where is the Servant
        who cares not for wage?
To Kiev she is gone
        on pilgrimage.

Yes, Anna went. The old man pled,
Mark almost wept for her to stay,
As mother sit, to see him wed.
Her call of duty elsewhere lay.

"No, Mark, such honor must I not take
To sit while you your homage make
To parents dear.
My mind is clear.
A servant must not thy mother be
Lest wealthy guests may laugh at thee.
Now may God's mercy with thee stay,
To the saints at Kiev I go to pray.
But yet again shall I return
Unto your house, if you do not spurn
My strength and toil."

With pure heart
        she blessed her Mark
And weeping, passed
        beyond the gate.

Then the wedding blossomed out;
Work for musicians and the joyous rout
Of dancing feet;
While mead so sweet
Of fermented honey with spices dashed
Over the benches and tables splashed,
Meanwhile the Servant limps along
Hastening on the weary road to Kiev.
To the city come, she does not rest,

Hires to a woman of the town;
For wages carries water.
You see she money, money needs
For prayers to Holy Barbara.
She water carries, never tarries,
And mighty store of pennies saves,
Then in the Lavra's awesome caves
She seeks the blessed wealth she craves.

From St. John she buys a magic cap,
For Mark she bears it;
And when he wears it,
For never a headache need he give e'er a rap.
And then St. Barbara gives her a ring,
To her new daughter back to bring.

'Fore all the saints
        she makes prostrations,
Then home returns
        having paid her oblations.

She has come back.
Fair Kate with Mark makes haste to meet her,
Far beyond the gate they greet her,
Then into the house they bring her,
Draw her to the table there
Quickly spread with choicest fare.
Her news of Kiev they now request,
While Kate arranges her couch for rest.

"Why do they love me,
Why this respect?
Dear God above me,
Do they suspect?
Nay, that's not so,
'Tis just goodness, I know."

And still the Servant her secret kept,
Yet from the hurt of her penance wept.

VI.

THREE times have the waters frozen
　　Thrice thawed at the touch of spring.
Three times did the Servant
From Kiev her store of blessings bring.
And each time gentle Katherine,
As daughter, set her on her way,
A fourth time led her by the mounds
Where many dear departed lay.
Then prayed to God for her safe return
For whom in absence her heart would yearn.

It was the Sunday of the Virgin,
Old Trophimus sat in garments white,
On the bench, in wide straw hat,
All amid the sunshine bright.
Before him with a little dog
His frolicsome grandson played,
The while his little granddaughter
Was in her mother's garb arrayed.
Smiling he welcomed her as matron;
For so at "visitors" they played.

"But what did you do with the visitor's
　　cake?
Did somebody steal it in the wood,
Or perhaps you've simply forgotten to
　　bake?"
For so they talked in lightsome mood.

But see,—Who comes?
'Tis their Anna at the door!
Run old and young! Who'll come before?
But Anna waits not their welcome wordy.

"Is Mark at home, or still on journey?"

"He's off on journey long enough,"
Says the old man in accents gruff.

With pain the Servant sadly saith,
"Home have I come with failing breath;
Nor 'mid strangers would I wait for death.
May I but live my Mark to see,
For something grievously weighs on me."

From little bag the children's gifts
She takes. There's crosses and amulets.
For Irene is of beads a string,
And pictures too, and for Karpon
A nightingale to sweetly sing,
Toy horses and a wagon.
A fourth time she brings a ring
From St. Barbara to Katherine.
Next the old man's gift she handles,
It's just three holy waxen candles.

For Mark and herself
       she nothing brought:
For want of money
       she nothing bought.

For want of strength
    more funds to earn,
Half a bun was her wealth
    on her return.
As to how to divide it
Let the babes decide it.

VII.

SHE enters now the house so sweet,
And daughter Katherine bathes her feet,
Then sets her down to dine in state,
But my Anna nor drank nor ate.

"Katherine!
When is our Sunday?"

"After tomorrow's the day."
"Prayers for the dead soon will we need
Such as St. Nicholas may heed.
Then we must an offering pay,
For Mark tarries on the way.
Perchance somewhere,
    from our vision hid,
Sickness has ta'en him
    which God forbid."
The tears dropped down
    from the sad old eyes,
So wearily did she
    from the table rise.

"Katherina,
My race is run,
All my earthly tasks are done.
My powers no longer I command
Nor on my feet have strength to stand.
And yet, my Kate, how can I die
While in this dear warm home I lie?"

The sickness harder grows amain,
For her the sacred host's appointed,
She's been with holy oils anointed,
Yet nought relieves her pain.
Old Trophim' in courtyard walks a-ring
Moving like a stricken thing.
Katherine, for the suff'rers sake
Doth never rest for her eyelids take,
And even the owls upon the roof
Of coming evil tell the proof.

The suff'rer now, each day, each hour,
Whispers the question, with waning power:
"Daughter Katherine, is Mark yet here?
So struggle I with doubt and fear,
Did I but know I'd see him for sure
Through all my pain I might endure."

VIII.

Now Mark comes on with the
    caravan
Singing blithely as he can.
To the inns he makes no speed,
Quietly lets the oxen feed.
Mark brings home for Katherine
Precious cloth of substance rich;
For father dear, a girdle sewn
Of silk so red.
For Servant Anne
    a gold cloth bonnet
To deck her head,
    And kerchief, too
      with white lace on it.
For the children are shoes
    with figs and grapes.
There's gifts for all,
    there's none escapes.
For all he brings
    red wine, so fine,
From great old city
    of Constantine.
There's buckets three
    in each barrel put on,
And caviar
    from the river Don.
Such gifts he has
    in his wagon there,
Nor knows the sorrow
    his loved ones bear.

On comes Mark,
            knows not of worry;
But he's come
            Give God the glory!
The gate he opens,
            Praising God.

"Hear'st thou, Katherine?
Run to meet him!
Already he's come,
Haste to greet him!
Quickly bring him in to me.
Glory to Thee, my Saviour dear,
All the strength has come from Thee.'

And she "Our Father" softly said
Just as if in dream she read.
The old man the team unyokes,
Lays away the carven yokes.
Kate at her husband strangely looks.

"Where's Anna, Katherine?
I've been careless!
She's not dead?"

            "No, not dead,
But very sick and calls for thee."

On the threshold Mark appears,
Standing there as torn by fears.
But Anna whispers, "Be not afraid,
Glory to God, Who my fears allayed.

Go forth, Katherine,
        though I love you well,
I've something to ask him,
        something to tell."

From the place
        fair Katherine went;
While Mark his head
        o'er the Servant bent.
"Mark, look at me,
Look at me well!
A secret now I have to tell.
On this faded form
        set no longer store,
No servant, I, nor Anna more,
I am——"
        Came silence dumb,
Nor yet guessed Mark
        What was to come.

Yet once again her eyelids raised
Into his eyes she deeply gazed
'Mid gathering tears.

"I from thee forgiveness pray;
I've penance offered day by day
All my life to serve another.
Forgive me, son, of me,
For I — am thy mother."

She ceased to speak.
A sudden faintness
     Mark did take:
It seemed the earth
     itself did shake.
He roused —
     and to his mother crept,
But the mother
     forever slept.

A Father's Legacy

When Gregory Shevchenko—for this was the father's name—was on his deathbed, he called his family around him and gave his parting bequests. A serf might not, indeed, sell any of his household goods without permission of his landlord, but he could give them to his relatives who, of course, were the property of the same landlord. So Gregory Shevchenko distributed his pitiful treasures to the children and to his wife,—saying finally—

"To my son, Taras, I give nothing. He will be no common man. Either he will be something very good or else a great rascal. For him the patrimony will either mean nothing, or will not help any."

Caucasus

To Jacques de Balmont—French friend of the Ukrainians who perished in the Circassian war.

The Czars used the Ukrainians as tools in their ambitious projects. A hundred thousand of them perished in the marshes, digging the foundations of Petrograd. As many more died in the attempt to subdue the Circassians—tribes inhabiting the Caucasus mountains—to the imperial will of the Russian autocrat.

The memory of these sufferings was the inspiration of this bitter poem.

The text is taken from the prophecy of Jeremiah, Chapter 9, verse 1.

"Oh, that my head were waters, and mine eyes a fountain of tears, that I might weep day and night for the slain of the daughter of my people."

BEYOND the hills are mightier hills,
   Cloud mountains o'er them rise,
Red, red have flowed their streams and rills,
They're sown with human woes and sighs.

There long ago in days of old
Olympus' Czar, the angry Jove,
His wrath did pour on a hero bold,
On brave Prometheus, he who strove
The fire of heaven to seize for men.

On mountain side, in vulture's den
He suffered what no mortal pen
May well indite. The savage beak
Of his hearts' blood doth daily reek.
Yet the torn heart again revives,
To triumph o'er its tortures strives.

Our souls yield not to grievous ills,
To freedom march our stubborn wills.
Though waves of trouble o'er us roll
The waves move not the steadfast soul.
Our living spirit is not in chains,
The word of God in glory reigns.

'Tis not for us to challenge Thee,
Though life rolls on in toil and tears;
Though we Thy purpose cannot see
We cling to hope 'mid doubts and fears.
Our cause lies sunk in drunken sleep
When will it awaken, Lord?

Oppressors gloat and patriots weep,
When wilt strength to us afford?

So weary, then art Thou, Oh God,
Can'st life to us no longer give?
Thy Truth we trust beneath the rod,
Believing in Thy strength we live.
Our cause shall rise,
Our freedom rise
Though tyrants rage:
To Thee alone,
All nations bow
Through age on age
And yet meantime
      the streams do flow
And ever tinged with blood
      they go.

Beyond the hills are mightier hills,
Cloud mountains o'er them rise.
Red, red have flowed their streams and rills,
They're sown with human woes and sighs.

Look at us in tender heartedness,
All in hunger dire and nakedness,
Forging freedom in unhappiness,
Toiling ever without blessedness.

The bones of soldiers bleaching lie,
In blood and tears must many die.

In faith, there's widows' tears, I think,
To all the Czars to give to drink.
Then there's tears of many a maiden
Falling so soft in the lonely night.
Hot tears of mothers, sorrow-laden,
Dry tears of fathers, in grievous plight.
Not rivers, but a sea has flowed,
A burning sea.
To all the Czars who in triumph rode,
With their hounds and gamekeepers,
Their dogs and their beaters,
May glory be!

To you be glory, hills of blue,
All clad in monstrous chains of frost.
Glory to you, ye heroes true,
With God your labors are not lost.
Fear not to fight, you'll win at length,
For you, God's ruth,
For you is freedom, for you is strength,
And Holy Truth.

TO THE CIRCASSIANS

"OUR bread and home," in your own tongue,
In Tartar words you dare to say.
Nobody gave it you, your world is young,
So far no one has ta'en it away.
Nobody yet has led you in fetters,
But we have wisdom in such matters.

In God's good word we daily read,
But from dungeons where the pris'ners moan,
To Caesar's high-exalted throne
'Tis gilt without, while the soul's in need.

To us for wisdom should you come,
We'll teach you all the tricks of trade.
Good Christians we, with church and Ikon:
All goods, even God, our own we've made.

But that house of yours
        Still hurts our eyes;
If we didn't give it,
        Why should you have it?
These ways of yours
        cause much surprise.
We never granted
        The corn you planted.
The sunlight, you
        Should pay for, too.
Oh, quite uneducated you!

Good Christians we, no pagans needy,
Sound in the faith, not a bit greedy.
If you in peace from us would learn
Store of wisdom you would earn.

With us what great illumination,
A cont'nent 'neath our domination;
Siberia great, for illustration.
There's jails and folks 'yond computation.

From Moldavia to Finlandia
Many tongues but nothing said,
Except for blessings on your head.

A holy monk here reads the Bible,
Tells the story, 'tis no libel,
Of king who stole his neighbour's wife,
And then the neighbour he robbed of life.
The king now dwells in paradise.
Such folks 'mong us to heaven rise.

Oh, you creatures unenlightened,
Be ye not of our dogmas frightened!
Our gentle art of "grab" we'll teach;
A coin to the church and heaven you'll reach.
Whatever is there we can't do?
The stars we count and crops we sow;
The foreigner curse,
Then fill our purse,
The people selling,
'Tis truth I'm telling.

No niggers we sell, I'm not making jokes,
Just common ord'nary Christian folks.
No Spaniards we, may God forbid!
Nor Jews that stolen goods have hid.
So don't you think you'd like to be
Such law-abiding folks as we?

TO THE RICH AND GREAT

IS it by the apostle's law
That ye your brother love?
Hypocrites and chatterers,
Ye're cursed of God above.

Not for your brother's soul you care.
It's only for his skin.
The skin from off his back you'd tear,
Some trifling prize to win.

There's furs for your daughter,
Slippers for your wife,
And things that you don't utter
About your private life.

TO THE MASTER

OH, wherefore wert Thou crucified,
　　Thou Christ, the Son of God?
That the word of Truth be glorified?
Or that we good folks should 'scape the rod
Of avenging wrath, by faith confest?
Meanwhile of Thee we make a jest,
Mocking Thy love in our conduct's test.

Cathedrals and chapels with Icons grand!
'Mid smoke of incense lavers stand.
There before Thy pictured Presence
Crowds unwearied make obeisance;
For spoil, for war, for slaughter seek
Their brother's blood to shed they pray,
And then before Thy form so meek
The loot of burning towns they lay.

AGAIN ADDRESSING THE CIRCASSIANS

THE sun on us has shone so bright,
  We wish to you to give the light.
That sun of truth we seek to show
To children blind, all in a row.
Wonders all to see we'll let you
If in our hands we only get you.
Of building jails we'll show the trick,
How pris'ners 'gainst their fetters kick.
There's knotted whips for stubborn backs,
For saucy nations painful racks.
In change for your mountains grand and old,
With this instruction we you greet.
These are the last things, already we hold
The plains and seas beneath our feet.

TO JACQUES DE BALMONT

SO they drove thee along, my dearest friend,
For Ukraina did'st thou shed
That good heart's blood of thine so red.
Our country's hangman, shame to think,
Muscovite poison gave thee to drink.
Oh, friend of mine, unforgotten friend,
Ukraine to thee doth welcome send.
Let thy spirit fly with Cossacks bold,
Along the shores of Dnieper old.
O'er ancient tombs hold watch and guard
And weep with us in labors hard.

Till I return to meet thee,
My songs I send to greet thee.
Such songs they are of bitter woe,
Yet ever, always, these I sow.

Thoughts and songs forever sowing,
To the care of winds bestowing.
Gentle winds of Ukraine
Shall bear them like the dew
To that dear land of mine
To greet my friends so true.

The Meaning of Serfdom

Three or four days of every week the serfs—men and women alike—must labor in their master's fields for nought. What was left of the week, they were granted to earn subsistence for themselves and their families.

But that was not the worst. More bitter than labor was the fact that they were not their own, were chattels of their lord, who could sell them at his pleasure or gamble them away at cards.

He could beat them too, or kill them if he wished, without fear, for what advocate would take up the case of a penniless serf against the all-powerful aristocracy.

Hideous, too, was the glaring fact that young daughters of the serfs were regarded as the legitimate prey of the landlord and his sons.

In these later days the sins of the fathers have been visited in awful fashion on the descendants of these landlords. But can we wonder that in the writings of a poet whose childhood was poisoned by knowledge of such injustice, we find evidence of the growing avenging fury that later was to bring about such awe-inspiring convulsions in human society.

Through all of Shevchenko's verse there sounds the great theme of that contrast between the beauty of God's world, and the horrors of human cruelty.

"An earthly heaven we had from Thee; Turned it into hell have we."

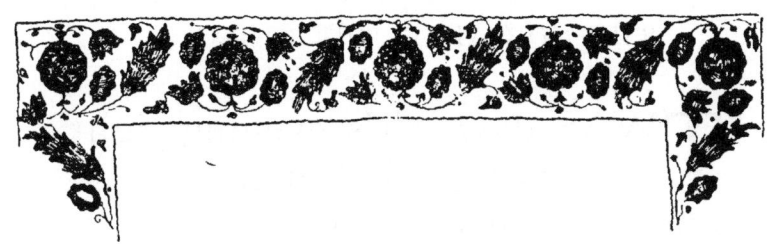

To the Dead

And the Living, and the Unborn, Countrymen of mine, in Ukraine, or out of it, My Epistle of Friendship.

This is the national poem of the Ukrainians, recited at all their gatherings. I have given the thought and something of the feeling. The music of the original I could not give. It begins like a Highland dirge with wailing amphibrachs, and there are other measures in it not used in our language. Perhaps some future student may be moved to put this poem in such English form as will give the true impression of the original.

The motive of the poem is, in part, to awaken the conscience of the young educated Ukrainians who, for the sake of gain were allowing themselves to be used as tools by foreign oppressors.

'TWAS dawn, 'tis evening light,
    So passes Day divine.
Again the weary folk
And all things earthly
    Take their rest.
I alone, remorseful
For my country's woes,
    Weep day and night,
By the thronged cross-roads,
Unheeded by all.
They see not, they know not;
Deaf ears, they hear not.
They trade old fetters for new
And barter righteousness,
Make nothing of their God.
They harness the people
With heavy yokes.
Evil they plough,
With evil they sow.
What crops will spring?
What harvest will you see?

Arouse ye, unnatural ones,
Children of Herod!
Look on this calm Eden,
Your own Ukraine,
Bestow on her tender love,
Mighty in her ruins.
Break your fetters,
Join in brotherhood.
Seek not in foreign lands

Things that are not.
Nor yet in Heaven,
Nor in stranger's fields,
But in your own house
Lies your righteousness,
Your strength and your liberty.

In the world is but one Ukraine,
Dnieper—there is only one.
But you must off to foreign lands
To look for something grand and good.
Wealth of goodness and liberty,
Fraternity and so forth, you found.
And back you brought to Ukraine
From places far away
A wondrous force
    of lofty sounding words,
And nothing more.
Shout aloud
    That God created you for this,
To bow the knee to lies,
To bend and bend again
    Your spineless backs
And skin again
    Your brothers—
These ignorant buckwheat farmers.

Try again
    to ripen crops of truth and light
In Germany
    or some other foreign place.
If one should add

>   all our present misery
> To the wealth
>   Our fathers stole
> Orphaned, indeed, would Dnieper be
>   with all his holy hills.
> Faugh! if it should happen
>   that you would never come back,
> Or get snuffed out
>   just where you were spawned
> No children would weep
>   nor mothers lament,
> Nor in God's house be heard
>   the story of your shame.
> The sun would not shine
>   on the stench of your filth
> O'er the clean, broad, free land,
> Nor would the people know
>   what eagles you were
> Nor turn their heads to gaze.

Arouse ye, be men!
For evil days come.
Quickly a people enchained
Shall tear off their fetters;
Judgment will come,
Dnieper and the hills will speak.
A hundred rivers
    flow to the sea
        with your children's blood,
Nor will there be any to help.

Smoke clouds hide the sun
Through the ages
    Your sons shall curse you.

Wash yourselves—
    The divine likeness in you
        defile not with slime.
Befool not your children
    that they were born to the world
        to be lordlings.
The eyes of men untaught
    see deep, deep
        into your soul.
Poor things they may be,
    yet they know the ass
        in the lion's skin.
And they will judge you,
    the foolish will pronounce the doom
        of the wise.

II.

Did you but study as you should,
You would possess your own wisdom;
And you might creep up to heaven.

But it is we—
      Oh, no, not we;
  It is I—no, no, not I.
I've seen it all, I know it.
There's neither heaven nor hell,
Not even God—
      Just I and the short, fat German.
      Nothing more.

Grand, my brother.
You ask me something,
    "I don't know,
        Ask the German,
        He'll tell you."
That's the way you learn
    in foreign lands.
The German says—
    "You are Mongols.
        Mongols, Mongols;
Naked children
    of the golden Tamerlane."
The German says—
    "You are Slavs,
        Slavs, Slavs;

Ugly offspring
    of famous ancestors."
You read the writings
    of the great Slavophils,
Push in among them,
    Get on so well
That you know all the tongues
    of the Slavonic peoples
Except your own—God help it.
"Oh, as for that·
    Sometime we'll speak
        our own language
When the German
    shows us how,
Our history too,
    he will explain,
Then we'll be alright!"
It came about finely
    on the German advice.
They learned to speak so well
        That even the mighty German
            could not understand them.
Not to speak of common folks.
Oh what a noise and racket!
"There's Harmony, and Force
And Music—and everything.
And as for History
The Epic of a free people!
What's all this about the poor Romans,
Brutus, etcetera, and the Devil knows what?
Have we not our Brutuses

   and our Cocles
Glorious and never to be forgotten?
Why freedom grew up with us
Bathed in the Dnieper
Rested her head on our hills,
The far-flung Steppes
   are her garments."
Alas! 'twas in blood she bathed
Pillowed her head on burial mounds
  On bodies of Cossack freemen,
   Corpses despoiled.
But look ye well
  Read again of that glory!
Read it, word by word,
Miss not a jot nor tittle,
Grasp it all:
  Then ask yourselves—
Who are we? Whose sons?
 Of what fathers?
   By whom and why enchained?
Then you shall see
  Who your glorious Brutuses are.
Slaves, door-mats!
  mud of Moscow
   scum of Warsaw
    are your lords;
Glorious heroes they are.
Why are you so proud
Sons of unhappy Ukraine.
That you go so well under the yoke?
Even better you go

than your fathers went.
Don't brag so much,
    they just skin you,
They rendered out your fathers' bones
Perhaps you are proud
    that your brotherhood
        has defended the faith.
You cooked your dough-nuts
    o'er the fires
        of burning Turkish towns,
of Sinope and Trebizond.
    True for you
        And you ate them
·And now they pain you,
And on your own fields
    the wily German
        plants potatoes.
You buy them from him,
    eat them for the good of your health
    and praise Cossackery.
But with whose blood
    was the land sprinkled
        that grew the potatoes?
Oh, that's a trifle;
    so long as it's good for the garden.
Very proud you are
    that we once destroyed Poland.
Very true indeed:
    Poland fell,
        but fell on top of us.

So your fathers shed their blood
    for Moscow and for Warsaw,
And left to you, their sons
    their fetters and their glory.

III.

To the very limit
    has our country come,
Her own children
    crucify her
      worse than the Poles.
How like beer
    they draw off
        her righteous blood.
They would, you see
    enlighten the maternal eyes
        with everlasting fires;
Lead on the poor blind cripple
    after the spirit of the age,
    German fashion!
Fine, go ahead,
    show us the way!
Let the old mother learn
    how to look after such children
Show away!
    For this instruction,
Don't worry—
    Good motherly reward will be.
The illusion fades
    from your greedy eyes
Glory shall you see,
    such glory as fits
        the sons of deceitful sires.

To study then, my brothers,
Think and read,

Learn from the foreigner
Despise not your own.
Who forgets his mother
Him God will punish.
Foreigners will despise him
Nor admit him to their homes;
His children shall as strangers be
Nor shall he find happiness on earth.
I weep when I remember
    the deeds of our fathers,
        deeds I can not forget.
Heavy on my heart they lie;
    Half my life I'd give
        could I forget them.
Such is our glory
    the glory of Ukraine.
So read then
    that ye may see
Not in dream
    but in vision
    All the wrongs that lie
        beneath yon mighty tombs.
Ask then of the martyrs
    by whom, when and for what
        were they crucified.
Embrace then
    brothers mine—
The least of your brethren.
That your mother may smile again,
Smile through her tears.

Give blessings to your children
   with hard toiler's hands;
With free lips kiss them
   when they are washed and clad.
Forget the shameful past
And the true glory shall live again,
   the glory of the Ukraine.
And clear light of day
   not twilight gloom
Shall gently shine.
Love one another, my brothers,
I pray you—I plead.

Freedom and Friends

With his new freedom Shevchenko finds himself in a different world. Not only does he meet the most brilliant people of the Russian Capital—scientists, artists, generals, nobles are his intimates. Count Tolstoi and Prince and Princess Repnin are his patrons.

He is introduced, too, in Russian or Polish translations to the great authors of other lands and times,—Greece and Rome, Germany and Britain offer him their treasures.

To us it is interesting to know that Byron, Walter Scott, and Shakespeare profoundly influenced him.

But a conflict of spirit now faces him. His worldly interests and his judgment advise him to go on with his painting. But strange music seems to ring in his ears. It is the music of his beautiful and suffering Ukraine. Songs seem to come to him from the wind and he writes them down.

They are in the peasant language of the Ukraine.

His 'Kobzar' appears in its first edition, with eight poems, in 1840. It is like a lightning flash through Russia.

Great Russian critics sneered at it, saying it was in the language of the swineherds. But the whole Ukraine recognized it as the voice of their suppressed nation. The down-trodden masses of all Russia knew that they had found a spokesman.

Shevchenko was now famous but he had chosen, without knowing it, 'The Way of the Cross.'

A Dream

This poem was written in 1847 in Siberia. Taken away suddenly from Ukraine, Shevchenko could not forget his motherland. His beloved Ukraine was very far from him, and he longed for her even in his dreams. He describes in the poem a dream which he had about the beauties of the Ukraine, which he had just left and which he never hoped to see again. The old man of whom he speaks represents the poet himself, who knew the miseries of his native land and who desired to spend the last hours of his life there.

OH my lofty hills—
　　Yet not so lofty
But beautiful ye are.
Sky-blue in the distance;
Older than old Pereyaslav,
Or the tombs of Vebla,
Like those clouds that rest
Beyond the Dnieper.

I walk with quiet step,
And watch the wonders peeping out.
Out of the clouds march silently
Scarped cliff and bush and solitary tree;
White cottages creep forth
Like children in white garments,
Playing in the valley's gloom.
And far below our gray old Cossack,
The Dnieper, sings musically
Amid the woods.
And then beyond the Dnieper on the hillside,
The little Cossack church
Stands like a chapel,
With its leaning cross.

Long it stands there, gazing, waiting,
For the Cossacks from the Delta;
To the Dnieper prattles,
Telling all its woe.
From its green-stained windows,
Like eyes of the dead,
It peeps as from the tomb.

Dost thou look for restoration?
Expect not such glory.
Robbed are thy people.
For what care the wicked lords
For the ancient Cossack fame?

And Traktemir above the hill
Scatters its wretched houses
Like a drunken beggar's bags.
And there is old Manaster
Once a Cossack town.
Is that the one that used to be?
All, all is gone, as a playground for the kings.
The land of the Zaporogues and the village
All, all the greedy ones have taken.
And you hills, you permitted it!
May no one look on you more
Cursed ones!—No! No!
Not you I curse,
But our quarreling generals,
And the inhuman Poles.

Forgive me, my lofty ones,
Lofty ones and blue,
Finest in the world, and holiest,
Forgive me, I pray God.
For so I love my poor Ukraina,
I might blaspheme the holy God,
And for her lose my soul.
On a curve of lofty Trektemir
A lonely cottage like an orphan stands,

Ready to plunge from off the height
To loved Dnieper, far below.
From that house Ukraina is seen,
And all the land of the Hetmans.
Beside the house an old gray father sits.
Beyond the river the sun goes down
As he sits, and looks, and sadly thinks.
"Alas, Alas!" the old man cries,
"Fools, that lost this land of God,
The Hetmans' land."
His brow with thought is clouded,
Something bitter he would have said
But did not.

"Much have I wandered in the world,
In peasant's coat and garb of lord.
How is it beyond the Ural,
Among the Kirghiz, Tartars?
Good God, even there it is better
Than in our Ukraina.
Perhaps because the Kirghiz
Are not Christians.
Much evil hast thou done, Oh Christ,
Hast changed the people God had made.
Our Cossacks lost their foolish heads
For truth, and the Christian faith.
Much blood they shed, their own and others.
And were they better for it?
Bah! No! They were ten times worse.
Apart from knife and auto-da-fe
They have chained up the people,

And they kill them.
Oh gentlemen, Christian gentlemen!"

My grey old man, with sorrow beaten,
Ceased, and bent his brave old head.
The evening sun gilded the woods,
The river and fields were covered with gold.
Mazeppa's cathedral in whiteness shines;
Great Bogdan's tomb is gleaming,
The willows bend o'er the road to Kiev,
And hide the Three Brothers' ancient graves.
Trubail and Alta, mid the reeds
Approach, unite in sisterly embrace.
Everything, everything gladdens the eyes,
But the heart is sad and will not see.
The glowing sun has bade farewell
To the dark land.
The round moon rises with her sister star,
Out they step from behind the clouds.
The clouds rejoiced
But the old man gazed,
And his tears rolled down.
"I pray Thee, merciful God,
Mighty Lord, Heavenly Judge,
Suffer me not to perish;
Grant me strength to overcome my woe,
To live out my life on these sacred hills;
To glorify Thee and rejoice in Thy beauty,
And at last, though beaten by the people's
    sins,

To be buried on these lofty hills,
And to abide on them."

He dried his tears,
Hot tears, though not the tears of youth;
And thought on the blessed years of long ago
Where was this?
What, how, and when?
Was it truth, or was it dream?
On what seas have I been sailing?
The green wood in the twilight,
The maiden with eyebrows dark,
The moon at rest among the stars,
The nightingale on the viburnum.
Whether in silence or in song
Praising the Holy God.
And all, all is in Ukraina.
The old man smiled—
Well, it may be—you can't avoid the truth
So it was—they wooed,
They parted, they did not marry.
She left him to live alone,
To live out his life.

The old man was sad again,
Wandered long about the house,
Then prayed to God,
Went in the house to sleep,
And the moon was swathed in clouds.

Thus in a foreign land
I dreamed my dream,
As if born again to the world
In freedom once more.
Grant me, Oh God, some time,
In old age, perchance,
To stand again on these stolen hills,
In a little cottage,
To bring my heart eaten out with sorrow
To rest at last, on the hills above the
  Dnieper.

A Triumphal March

In 1845 Shevchenko was graduated from the Imperial Academy of Arts at Petersburg. Shortly after he travelled to the Ukraine, purposing to devote his life to the service of his own people.

His progress was a triumphal march, a succession of banquets and popular welcomes and entertainments at the homes of the wealthy.

At Kiev people still remember that the earliest Russian civilization had its beginnings in the Ukraine. There christianity first took root, and there were the first Russian Princes.

Before Shevchenko's arrival there was organized at Kiev the Society of Cyril and Methodius, called after the great apostles of Russia, and the leading spirits of the Society were professors in the University of Kiev.

Into this brilliant company Shevchenko was welcomed. Its leaders became his devoted friends. A chair of painting in the University was to be established for him.

Most remarkable were the relations between Shevchenko and Professor Kulisch.

Kulisch was to be married to a great lady, a daughter of one of the nobles of the country. The poet was invited to the wedding and the bride, in her enthusiasm, actually kissed his hand. This was an astonishing act of condescension towards one who had been a serf, but this lady, herself afterwards a famous authoress, cherished the memory to her dying day.

Shevchenko's saddest experience in the Ukraine was when he visited his native village and found his brothers and sisters in serfdom. His dream was to earn enough money to purchase their freedom, and afterwards to devote his life to the liberation of the peasantry. The poem—"The Bondwoman's Dream" — commemorates the poet's meeting with his favorite sister, Katherine, working as a slave.

His friends thought he should go to Italy to perfect himself in painting. Madame Kulisch purposed to sell her family jewels to raise sufficient money to send Shevchenko to that country. Her husband who was in the plot told Shevchenko that some wealthy person had contributed the money but he must not ask for the donor's name.

But on returning to Kiev from the Kulisch home a policeman put his hand on the shoulder of the poet painter.

The bright dream was ended.

Shevchenko meets his sister.

The Bondwoman's Dream

THE slave with sickle
    reaped the wheat,
Then wearily limped
    among the stooks;
But not to rest,
Her little son she sought
Who wakened crying
    in cool nest
        among the sheaves.
His swaddled limbs unwrapped
    she nourished him,
Then, dandling him a moment
    fell asleep.
In dreams she saw
    her little son,
Her Johnny, grown to man,
    handsome and rich.
No lonely bachelor
    but a married man
In freedom it seemed,
    no longer the landlord's
        but his own man.

And in their own joyous field
    his wife and he
        reaped their own wheat.
Their children brought their food.
    The poor thing
        laughed in her sleep,
Woke up—
    a dream indeed it was.
She looked at Johnny,
    picked him up and swaddled him,
And back to her allotted task;
Sixty stooks her stint.
Perhaps the last of the sixty it was:
    God grant it.
And God grant
    this dream of thine
        may be fulfilled.

Shevchenko's birthplace.

To the Makers of Sentimental Idyls.

DID you but know, fine dandy,
　　The people's life of misery
You would not use such pretty phrases,
Nor give to God such empty praises.
At our tears you're laughing,
And our sorrows chaffing,
Slave's cot in a shady spot—
You call it heaven! Rot!
I lived once in such a shanty,
Of childhood's tears I shed a plenty.
In bitter sorrows we were wise,
Home that you call paradise.

No paradise I call thee,
Little cottage in the wood,
With the water pure beside thee
Close by the village rude!
There my mother bore me,
Singing she tended me;
My child's heart drank in her pain.

Cottage in the shady dell,
Heaven outside, inside hell;

But slavery there,
    with labor weary,
Nor time for prayer
    in life so dreary.

My mother good to her early grave
Was hurled by sorrows wave on wave.

The father weeping o'er his young,
    (little and naked were we),
Sank 'neath the weight of fated wrong
And died in slavery.
The children, we, of home bereft
Like little mice 'mong neigbors crept.

Water drawer was I at school,
My brothers toiled 'neath landlord's rule.

For my sisters an evil fate must be,
Though little doves they seemed to me;
Into life as serfs they're born,
And die they must in that lot forlorn.

I shudder yet, where'er I roam,
When I think of life in that village home.

Evil-doers, Oh God, are we,
An earthly heaven we had from Thee,
Turned it into hell have we,
And a second heaven is now our plea.

Gently we live with our brothers now,
With their lives our fields we plough;
Fields that with their tears are wet,
And yet—
What do we know?
	yet it seems as if Thou!
(For without Thy will
Should we suffer ill?)
Dost Thou, Oh Father in heaven holy
Laugh at us the poor and lowly?
Advise with them of noble birth
How so cleverly to rule the earth?

For see the woods their branches waving,
And there beyond, the white pool gleaming
And willows o'er the water bending,
Garden of Eden it is in sooth,
But of its deeds enquire the truth.

This wondrous earth should tell a story
Of endless joy, and praise, and glory
To Thee, Oh God, unique and holy.
Unhallowed spot,
Whence praise comes not!
A world of tears where curses rise,
To heaven above the hopeless skies.

Autocrat Versus Poet

Nicholas I was brought up in the traditions of autocracy and believed in them with all his heart. He hated liberal thought and detested the idea of educating the masses.

Tens of thousands of copies of the New Testament and the Psalter were burned by his orders. He said such books were for the priests, not for the common people. Incidentally it may be remarked that the priests had to teach what he wanted or lose their jobs.

To speak against his government, or even to criticize czars who reigned hundreds of years before him was a crime.

The little band of dreamers who formed the Society of Cyril and Methodius actually hoped to convert this autocrat, and secure his assistance in freeing the people. They had visions of a free Confederation of Slavonic states, after the pattern of the United States of America, but with the czar as head. But they sadly misjudged their man.

Shechenko had actually spoken impertinently of the Autocrat in his poems. He refused to retract.

The government really wished to be lenient, if he would only be good and confess that he had done wrong. But Shevchenko was not of those who are willing to admit that black is white.

The gloomy autocracy now pronounces his doom—a sort of living death in Siberian barracks. The czar added to the sentence, with his own hand, the proviso that he should not be allowed either to write or to paint.

A Poem of Exile

I COUNT in prison the days and nights
  And then forget the count.
How heavily, Oh Lord,
Do these days pass!
And the years flow after them,
Quietly they flow,
Bearing with them
Good and ill.
Everything do they gather
Never do they return.
You need not plead,
Your prayers unanswered fall.
Mid oozy swamps
    among the weeds
Year after weary year
    has sadly flowed.
Much of something have they taken
From dark store-house of my heart;
Borne it quietly to the sea,
    As quietly the sea swallowed it.
Not gold and silver
    Did they take from me,
But good years of mine
    Freighted with loneliness,

Sorrows written on the heart
    With unseen pen.
And a fourth year passes
    So gently, so slowly,
The fourth book
    of my imprisonment
I start to stitch up,
Embroidering it with tears
    Of homesickness
        in a foreign land.
Yet such woe
    tells itself not in words.
Never, never
    in the wide world.
In far away captivity
    There are no words
Not even tears,
    Just nothingness;
Not even God above thee,
Nothing is there to see,
None with whom to speak.
Not even desire for life.
Yet thou must live!
I must! I must!
    But for what?
That I may not lose my soul?
My soul is not worth
    such suffering!
Then why must I live on
    in the world,

Drag these fetters
 in my jail?
Because, perchance,
 my own Ukraine
I shall see again.
Again I shall pour out
 my words of sorrow
To the green groves
 and rich meadows.
No family have I of my own
 in all Ukraine,
Yet the people there
 are different from these foreigners
I would walk again
 among the bright villages
On the Dnieper's banks
 and sing my thoughts
  gentle and sad.
Grant me,
 Oh God of mercy
That I may live
 to see again
Those green meadows,
 those ancestral tombs.
If Thou wilt not grant this,
 Yet bear my tears
To my Ukraine.
 Because, God,
I die for her.
It may be that I shall lie
 more lightly in foreign soil

When sometimes in Ukraine
    they speak of my memory.
Carry my tears then
    Oh God of loving kindness,
Or at least
    send hope into my soul.
I can think no more
    with my poor head,
For coldness of death
    comes on me
When I think that they may
    bury me in foreign soil
And bury my thoughts with me
    And none tell about me
        in the Ukraine.

And yet it may be
    that gently through the years
My tear-embroidered songs
    shall fly sometime
And fall
    as dew upon the ground
On the tender heart of youth,
And youth shall nod assent.
And weep for me
Making mention of me in its prayers.
Well, as it will be
    so it will be.
Perhaps 'twill swim
    Perhaps 'twill wade
Yet even if they crucify me for it
I'll still write my verses.

Siberian Exile

Now-a-days we have many discussions and searchings of heart over the question of prisons and the purpose of punishment. I doubt if the autocracy suffered many qualms of conscience in such matters. It was simply an affair of silencing a dangerous voice and disciplining an unruly subject.

They were too humane to put him to death, they merely sought to crush his spirit. But the Slav spirit is hard to crush. It may brood and smoulder long, but sometime or other it will burst out in flames.

In the case of Shevchenko another influence may be seen at work. In his ragged youth, when acting as assistant to a drunken church singer he gained at least one thing. That was a familiarity with the Psalter and the Hebrew prophets. The deep religious fire of the Hebrew seems fused with his own irrepressible native genius to form a spirit that could not be subdued.

They tried to make a soldier of him but he could not or would not learn the tricks of the soldier's trade.

They forbade him to write but he wrote verses secretly and concealed them.

Occasionally a humane commander would relax the severity of the rules. One governor allowed him as a hidden favor the reading of the Bible and Shakespeare.

At another time he was taken with a scientific expedition to the Sea of Aral, and employed in the congenial task of painting the wild scenery of that part.

At other times again the severity would be redoubled and pen, ink and paper would be forbidden. Through it all his love and sorrow for his native land increased. Only the remembrance of Ukraine kept him alive.

Ten years of Siberia changed the gay young artist of bright eyes and abundant locks to a gray-bearded, bald-headed old man on whom Death had set his seal.

But his spirit was still unconquered. At the end of his imprisonment he wrote the "Goddess of Fame" and the "Hymn of the Nuns" to show it.

Memories of Freedom

Memories of Freedom
Bring sweet sadness to the exile's heart
And so lost liberty of mine
I dream of thee.
Never hast thou seemed to me
So fresh and young
And so surpassing fair
As now in this foreign land.
Alas! Alas!
Freedom that I sang away
Look at me from o'er the Dnieper,
Smile at me from there.
And thou my only love
Risest o'er the sea so far.
In the mist thy face appears
Like the evening star.
With thee, my only one
Thou bring'st my youthful years.
Before me like a sea—
Hamlets fair in broad array,
Cherry orchards, joyous crowds.
This the village, This the people
Who once as brothers
Welcomed me.
Mother! Dear old mother!
Home of memories fond!
Happy guests of days gone by!

Who gathered there in days gone by
Simply to dance in the good old way
From evening light till dawn.
Do sun-burned youth
And happy maidenhood
Still dance in the dear old home?
And thou, sweetheart of mine,
Thou heartsease of mine,
My sacred, dark-eyed one!
Still amongst them dost thou walk
Silent and proud?
And with those blue-black eyes
Still dost bewitch
    the peoples' souls?
Still as of old
Do they admire in vain
Thy supple form?
Goddess mine! fate of mine!
How wee maidens
Gather round thee,
Chirping and prattling
In the good old way.

Perchance, unwittingly,
The children remember me,
One makes a little jest of me.
Smile, my heart!
Just a little, little smile
That no one sees.
That's all. I, worse luck!
Must pray to God in jail.

A Scene from Siberia. Shevchenko's painting.

Memories of an Exile

MEMORIES of mine,
    Memories of home,
Sole wealth of mine,
    Where'er I roam.
When sorrows lower
In evil hour
And griefs o'ertake me
You'll not forsake me.
    From the land of my early loves
You will fly like grey-winged doves
From broad Dnieper's shore
O'er the steppes to soar.
Here the Kirghiz Tartars
Dwell naked in poverty.
They're wretched as martyrs
Yet this is their liberty;
To God they may pray
And none say them nay.
Will you but fly to meet me,
With gentle words
    I'll greet ye.
Of my heart
    ye children dear
O'er past loves
    we'll shed a tear.

Death of the Soul

As the nights pass, so pass the days,
    The year itself passes.
Again I hear the rustling
    of autumn leaves.
The light of the eyes is fading,
Memory is in the heart asleep.
Everything sleeps,
    and I know not
If I live or am already dead.
For so, aimless
    I wander in the world
No longer weep nor laugh.

Fate, where art thou?
    Fate, where art thou?
There's none of any sort!
Dost grudge me good fate,
    Oh God,
Then send it bad, as bad.
Leave me not
    to a walking sleep.
With heart like bears'
    in wintry den,
Nor yet like rotten log
    on earth to lie;
But give me to live,

with the heart to live,
And love the people.
If you won't
Let me curse them
and burn up the world.

Terrible it is to fall
into dungeons
Yet much worse—to sleep
And sleep and sleep
in freedom;
To slumber for an eternity
And leave not a footprint behind.
All alike—
whether one lives or dies.
Fate where art thou?
Fate where art thou?
There's none of any sort!
Dost grudge me good fate, Oh God,
Then give me bad, as bad.

Hymn of Exile

THE sun goes down beyond the hill,
　　The shadows darken, birds are still;
From fields no more come toiler's voices
In blissful rest the world rejoices.
With lifted heart I, gazing stand,
Seek shady grove in Ukraine's land.
Uplifted thus, 'mid memories fond
My heart finds rest, o'er the hills beyond.
On fields and woods the darkness falls
From heaven blue a bright star calls,
The tears fall down. Oh, evening star!
Hast thou appeared in Ukraine far?
In that fair land do sweet eyes seek thee
Dear eyes that once were wont to greet me?
Have eyes forgotten their tryst to keep?
Oh then, in slumber let them sleep
No longer o'er my fate to weep.

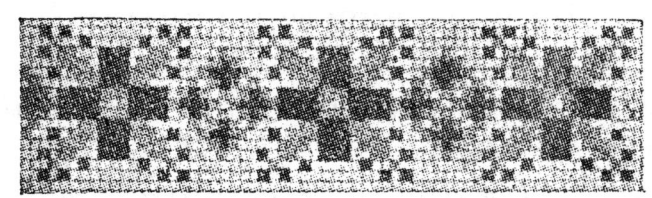

Returning Home

After a while a new Ceasar came to the throne, a man who was thought to have liberal tendencies.

Shevchenko's friends at once busied themselves with efforts for his release. Finally amnesty was granted. Count Tolstoi, on receiving the news late at night, hastened to waken his household and there was a family jubilation.

But the new autocrat, though somewhat benevolently inclined, was also a little bit suspicious. The banished poet was a pretty dangerous character. He had even disturbed the conscience of autocracy itself, hence he was only allowed to approach his home country by degrees. Finally he was allowed to reside in Petrograd and later even in Ukraine, welcomed everywhere by loving and pitying friends.

His wish for his old age was to inhabit a little cottage on the Dnieper's banks. For this purpose he purchased a piece of land on one of those hills so often referred to in his poems.

Death came too soon, however, but the property served as the site of his last resting place. He died at Petrograd but in the spring his remains were carried the long distance to his old home. A mourning people lined the way.

Only a couple of days after the poet's death, appeared the ukase of the czar proclaiming the abolition of serfdom. To the common people it seemed that their peasant poet, by his songs and his sufferings, had been the prime cause of their new freedom.

No speeches were allowed at the interment on the hill above the Dnieper but there were many people and many wreaths of flowers.

One wreath, deposited by a lady, expressed more than anything else the common feeling. That wreath was a crown of thorns.

On the Eleventh Psalm

MERCIFUL God, how few
  Good folk remain on earth.
Behold, each one in heart
Is setting snares for another.
But with fine words,
And lips honey-sweet
They kiss—and wait
To see how soon
Their brother to his grave
Will find his way.

But Thou who art Lord alone
Shuttest up the evil lips,
That great-speaking tongue
That says:—
    "No trifling thing are we,
How glorious shall we show
In intellect and speech.
Who is that Lord
    that will forbid
Our thoughts and words?"

Yea, the Lord shall say to Thee
"I shall arise, this day
On their behalf—
    People of mine in chains,

The poor and humble ones
    These will I glorify.
Little, dumb and slaves are they,
Yet on guard about them
    Will I set my Word."

Like trampled grass
Shall perish your thoughts
And words alike.

Like silver, hammered, beaten,
Seven times melted o'er the fire,
Are thy words, Oh Lord.
Scatter these holy words of Thine,
O'er all the earth,
That Thy children
    little and poor
May believe in miracles on earth.

Prayer I.

TO Tsars and kings
 who tax the world,
Send dollars and ducats,
And fetters well-forged.

To toiling heads and toiling hands,
Laboring on these stolen lands
Endurance and strength.

To me, my God, on this sad earth,
Give me but love,
 the heart's paradise
And nothing more.

Prayer II.

✦✦✦

MY prayer for the Tsars,
    These traffickers in blood,
That Thou on them would'st put
    Fetters of iron, in dungeons deep.

My prayer for the peoples
    toiling long,
Do Thou to them
    on their ravaged lands.
Send down Thy strength
    most merciful One.
And for the pure in heart
    Grant angel guards beside them,
To keep them pure.

And for myself, Oh Lord,
I ask nought else
But truth on earth to love,
And one true friend
    to love me.

Prayer III.

FOR those that have done wrong
    to me,
No longer do I fetters ask,
Nor dungeons deep.

For hands that faithful toil for good
Send Thy instructions' gracious aid,
And Holy strength.

For tender ones,
        the pure in heart
Do Thou, Oh God,
        their virtue save
With angel's guard.

For all Thy children on this earth
May they Thy wisdom
        know alike,
In brother love.

Prayer IV.

TO those of the ever-greedy eyes,
　Gods of earth, The Tsars,
Are the ploughs and the ships,
And all good things of earth
For these little gods.

To toiling hands,
To toiling brains
Is given to plough the barren field,
To think, to sow, and take no rest
And reap the fields anon.
Such the reward of toiling hands.

For the true-hearted lowly ones,
Peace-loving saints,
Oh, Creator of heaven and earth,
Give long life on earth,
And paradise beyond.

All good things of earth
Are for these gods, the Tsars,
Ploughs and ships,
All wealth of earth
For us—good lack!
Is left to love our brothers.

Mighty Wind

MIGHTY wind, mighty wind!
　　With the sea thou speakest;
Waken it, play with it,
　　Question the blue sea.
It knows where my lover is,
　　Far away it bore him.
It will tell, the sea will tell,
　　What it has done with him.

If it has drowned my darling,
　　Beat on the blue sea.
I go to seek my loved one,
　　And to drown my woe.
If I find him, I'll cling to him,
　　On his heart I'll faint.
Then waves bear me with him
　　Where'er the winds do blow.

If my lover is beyond the sea,
　　Mighty wind, thou knowest
Where he goes, what he does,
　　With him thou speakest.

If he weeps, then I shall weep,
  If not, I sing.
If my dark-haired one has perished,
  I shall perish, too.

Then bear my soul away
  Where my loved one is,
Plant me as a red viburnum
  On his tomb.
Better that an orphan lie
  In a stranger's field,
Over him his sweetheart
  Will bud and bloom.

As a blossom of viburnum
  Over him I'll bloom,
That foreign sun may burn him not,
  Nor strangers trample on his tomb.
At even I'll grieve,
  In the morning I'll weep.
The sun comes up,
  My tears I'll dry,
And no one sees.

Mighty wind, mighty wind!
  With the sea thou speakest.
Waken it, play on it,
  Question the blue sea.

The Water Fairy

ME my mother bore
  'Mid lofty palace walls,
Me at midnight hour
  In Dnieper's flood she bathed;
And bathing, she murmured
  Over little me:

  "Swim, swim, little maid,
  Adown the Dnieper water,
  You'll swim out a fairy
  Next midnight, my daughter.
  I go to dance with him,
  My faithless lover;
  You'll come and lure him
  Into the river.
  No more shall he laugh at me,
  At my tears out-flowing,
  But o'er him the Dnieper
  It's blue water is rolling.
  Swim out, my only one,
  He will come to dance with thee.
  Waves, waves, little waves,
    Greet ye the water fairy."

Sadly she cried and ran away,
As I floated down the stream.

But sister fairies met me,
I grew as in a dream.
A week, and I dance at midnight,
And watch from the water pools.
What does my sinful mother?
Lives she still in shameful pleasure,
With him, the faithless lord?
Thus the fairy whispered,
Then like diving bird she dropped
Back in the stream,
And the willows bowed above her.

The mother comes to walk by the river side.
'Tis weary in the palace,
And the lord is not at home.
   She comes to the bank, thinks of her little one
Whom she plunged in with muttered charms.
   What matters it? She would go back to the palace,
But no, her's is another fate.
   She noticed not how the river maidens hastened
Till they caught her, and tickled her 'mid laughter.
   Joyfully they caught her, and played and tickled her,
And put her in a basket net
  (Unto her death).
And then they roared and laughed;
But one little fairy did not laugh.

Hymn of the Nuns

❖❖❖❖

Shevchenko had heard a story of nuns in a convent conveying messeges to one another interspersed in the words of the religious service. The messeges were to the effect that company was coming that night and there would be music and dancing. Hence this sardonically humorous poem.

STRIKE lightning above this house,
This house of God where we are dying.
Where we think lightly of Thee, God,
And, thinking lightly, sing
      Hallelujah.

Were it not for Thee,
      we had loved men;
Had courted and married,
Brought up children,
Taught them and sung
      Hallelujah.

Thou hast cheated us,
      poor wretches!
And we, defrauded and unlucky,
Ourselves have fooled Thee,
And howled and sung: Hallelujah.

With barber's shears hast put us in this
      nunnery,
And we—young women still—
We dance and sing,
And singing say: Hallelujah.

To the Goddess of Fame

❖❖❖❖

HAIL, thou barmaid slovenly,
    Stagg'ring like fish-wife drunkenly;
Where the dickens dost thou stay,
With thy stock of haloes, pray?
Was it on credit thou gavest one
To the thief of Versailles, that Corsican?
Perhaps now thou'rt whispering in some
    fellow's ear;
And all because of boredom or beer.

Come then awhile with me to lodge,
Fondly, together, trouble we'll dodge.
With a smack and a kiss
    This dreary weather,
Let's make a bargain
    to live together.
Thou'rt a painted queen
    with manners free,
Yet in thy company
    I'd gladly be.

What though thou holdest
    thy nose in air,
Dancest in barrooms
    with kings at a fair;

And most with that chap
                they call the Tsar;
Still that's no bother,
                thy stock's still at par..

Come, my dear, make haste to me,
Let me have a look at thee;
Bestow on me a little smile,
'Neath thy bright wings
                I'd rest a while.

Iconoclasm

BRIGHT light, peaceful light,.
　　Free light, light unbound!
What is this, brother light?
In thy warm home thou'rt found
By censers smoked,
By priests' robes choked,
Fettered and fooled
And by Ikons ruled.
Yield thee not in the fight,
Waken up, brother light!
Shed thy pure rays
On mankind's ways.
All priestly robes in rags we'll tear
And light our pipes from censers rare,
With Ikons now the flames will roar,
With holy brooms we'll sweep the floor.

My Testament

WHEN I die, remember, lay me
    Lowly in the silent tomb,
Where the prairie stretches free,
    Sweet Ukraine, my cherished home.

There, 'mid meadows' grassy sward,
    Dnieper's waters pouring
May be seen and may be heard,
    Mighty in their roaring.

When from Ukraine waters bear
    Rolling to the sea so far
Foeman's blood, no longer there
    Stay I where my ashes are.

Grass and hills I'll leave and fly.
    Unto throne of God I'll go,
There in heaven to pray on high,
    But, till then, no God I know.

Standing then about my grave,
    Make ye haste, your fetters tear!
Sprinkled with the foeman's blood
    Then shall rise your freedom fair.

Then shall spring a kinship great,
    This a family new and free.
Sometimes in your glorious state,
    Gently, kindly, speak of me.